THE BIG
JOURNAL
FOR ANXIOUS
PEOPLE

THE BIG JOURNAL FOR ANXIOUS PEOPLE

Jordan Reid and Erin Williams

A TarcherPerigee Book

tarcherperigee

An imprint of Penguin Random House LLC
penguinrandomhouse.com

Most TarcherPerigee books are available at special quantity discounts for bulk purchase for sales promotions, premiums, fund-raising, and educational needs. Special books or book excerpts also can be created to fit specific needs. For details, write: SpecialMarkets@ penguinrandomhouse.com.

ISBN 9780593539507
Library of Congress Control Number: 2022934825

Printed in the United States of America
1st Printing

Book design by Jordan Reid and Erin Williams

Based on the series by Jordan Reid and Erin Williams

THIS BOOK BELONGS TO:

_____

_____

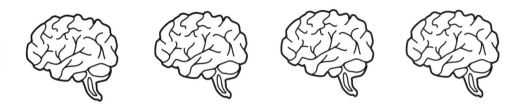

Dear Anxious Person,

Hello, and welcome to your brand-new journal.

Let us begin by apologizing for taking the liberty of addressing you as "Anxious Person." We don't even know you! It's just that we're comfortable making the following assumptions. You are:
   a) Human,
   b) Living on planet Earth, and
   c) Participating, whether passively or actively, in one or more
      forms of social media.

If the foregoing conditions are met, in accordance with the Premack principle* we must conclude that yes, you are anxious. Sorry.

Also, not sorry! Because there are plenty of other humans on planet Earth right this very minute and most of them are worrying about everything from airplane bathrooms to unanticipated phone calls to whether Carol washed her hands before grabbing that Snickers from the candy bowl because *she never does.*

God *damn* it, Carol.

Anxiety, in other words, is everywhere—and so are people who want to advise you on the best way to handle it ("just relax" being our favorite adage). Options for relieving the more

* Googled it.

uncomfortable by-products of anxiety are as varied as the sources of anxiety themselves. Some people reach for crystals, some for prescriptions, some for trips to Disneyland so frequent that their friends feel weird about it. Still others reach for—yes—a journal.

Whether you're new to journaling or have stacks of mortifying teenage musings hidden in your garage, this book is for you. In these pages, you'll find prompts to explore your feelings, confront your fears, and answer questions like "Should I doodle?" (Yes); "Is mainlining espresso a good idea?" (No); and "How can I never, ever, ever again think about how much money Kylie Jenner has?" (If you figure it out, DM us).

So relax (or don't), pick up the writing instrument of your choice, and flip the page to embark on a glorious journey of self-discovery, gratitude, and mindfulness, plus a healthy dose of lowered expectations, a dash of vengeance, and one very anxious cucumber. (You'll see.)

Love,
Jordan & Erin

still smiling   dead serious

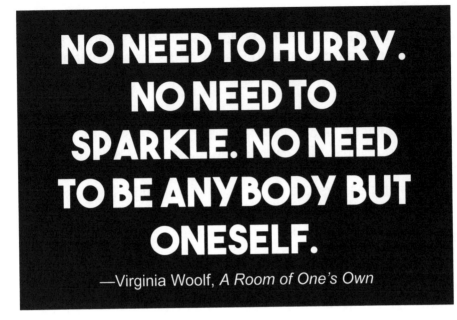

> # NO NEED TO HURRY. NO NEED TO SPARKLE. NO NEED TO BE ANYBODY BUT ONESELF.
>
> —Virginia Woolf, *A Room of One's Own*

Oh look, it's the first page of your journal!

Depending on your state of mind, this might make you feel anything from excited to overwhelmed to narcoleptic. So, how are you feeling about your decision to own, and engage with, a book called The Big Journal for Anxious People*?*

Before we move forward, let's get to know your wonderful, unique, and, sure, also anxious self a touch better.

≡ *LIGHTNING ROUND*

Where's your favorite place to be? _____

What place makes your entire body
cringe, because #justno? _____

Who are your favorite people?

_____

Who makes you absolutely insane
(besides Elon Musk, obviously)?

_____

What's your favorite thing to eat?

_____

What food needs to be evicted from
the earth?

_____

What's your favorite thing to do
outside?

_____

What sport would you not participate
in even upon pain of death?

_____

What's your favorite breakfast?

_____

What breakfast would you happily
replace with a bowl of dandruff
(besides Grape-Nuts)?

_____

What's your favorite way to chill out?

_____

What solo hobby is oh *hell* no, so not
your thing?

_____

What's your favorite quality in a
person?

_____

What's a personality quirk that
makes you want to scream?

_____

Who/what/where in the world makes
you feel most like yourself?

_____

I'VE GOT 99 PROBLEMS AND 86 OF THEM ARE COMPLETELY MADE-UP SCENARIOS IN MY HEAD THAT I'M STRESSING ABOUT FOR ABSOLUTELY NO LOGICAL REASON.

—UNKNOWN

Jay Z approves
this message*

Ever tried to remember your iCloud password? Yeah, we all have problems. The good news is that most of the things we worry about are actually not the world-enders we might think (unless you're storing the nuclear codes on your iCloud, in which case, please make an appointment with your local Genius Bar STAT, thanks).

What are some things that you're worried about right now that are completely out of your control?

_____

_____

_____

_____

_____

_____

_____

_____

_____

_____

_____

Leave them right here, on this page. You can pick them back up tomorrow if you still need to.

* Not really

NORMAL?
NAH.

Are you weird? Hooray for you! What does "normal" really mean, anyway?

"Boring." It means "boring."

What are five weird things about you?

_____

_____

_____

_____

_____

Why do these things make you so awesome?!*

_____

_____

_____

_____

* You are awesome.

BEING CALLED "WEIRD" IS LIKE BEING CALLED "LIMITED EDITION." MEANING YOU'RE SOMETHING PEOPLE DON'T SEE ALL THAT OFTEN. REMEMBER THAT.

—UNKNOWN

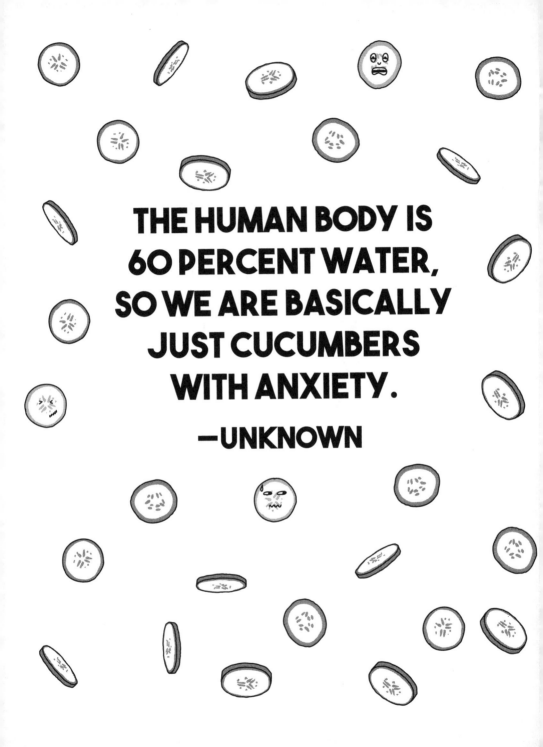

**THE HUMAN BODY IS
60 PERCENT WATER,
SO WE ARE BASICALLY
JUST CUCUMBERS
WITH ANXIETY.**

—UNKNOWN

MAKE THIS AN ANXIOUS CUCUMBER.

A CASE OF THE ANXIETY POOPS

Does anxiety make you need to poop? Congratulations, you are a human person.*

How does your body feel when you're anxious?

_____

_____

Where do you feel anxiety most acutely?

_____

_____

What was your pre-test ritual during high school/college? Did it involve pooping, like, a lot?

_____

_____

What's something you can do to release anxiety from your body? Deep breathing? Drinking something warm? Spending some time on omfgdogs.com?**

_____

_____

*This has an evolutionary basis. Pooping a lot makes you lighter, so you can run away from the scary performance review—err, saber-toothed tiger—faster. (Fine, it's your digestive enzymes reacting to your neuroendocrine system. But we like the pooping-makes-you-run-faster theory better.)

**Go there right now. It is magical.

CIRCLE ALL THE PLACES WHERE ANXIETY SHOWS UP IN YOUR BODY

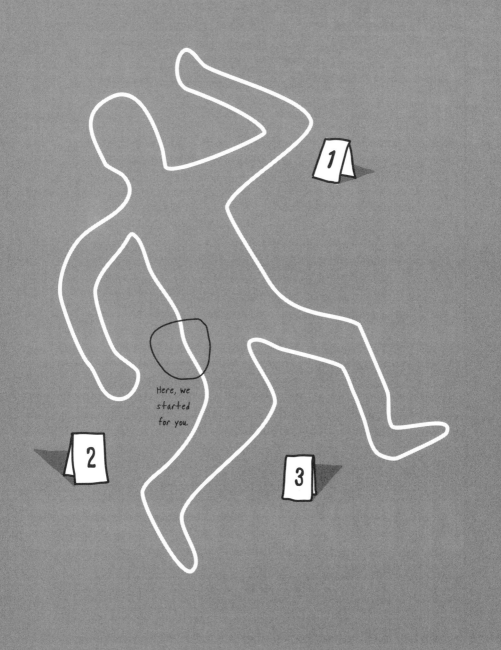

Because anxiety has a distinct evolutionary purpose—to help keep the human species alive—it's not all *bad. Maybe your anxiety sends you into productivity overdrive (thanks, adrenaline!) and helps you get shit done, or maybe it's just excellent at stopping you from trying to pet poisonous snakes (also a good idea).*

What are some not-too-terrible side effects of your anxieties?

_____

_____

_____

_____

_____

What heroic feat has your anxiety recently performed for you?

_____

_____

_____

_____

_____

If your anxiety were exiled to Krypton, is there anything you would miss about it?

_____

_____

_____

_____

DOODLE IT OUT

Doodling! A fun way to pass the time while Mom gives you a full over-the-phone recap of the reality show that you don't watch and, seriously, Mom, LITERALLY NEVER HAVE.

Go for it.

THE DOODLE IS THE BROODING OF THE HAND.

—SAUL STEINBERG

> ## I USED TO BE AFRAID OF THE DARK BECAUSE I THOUGHT THE MONSTERS WOULD GET ME. THEN ONE DAY I THOUGHT TO MYSELF, "MAYBE NOT ALL OF THE MONSTERS ARE BAD."
>
> ### —UNKNOWN

Anxiety can be overwhelming; we know this. Sometimes it even feels like a creature has invaded and taken over our brain, our body, our emotions.

Let's run with that. Close your eyes and picture your anxiety as a monster. Is it spiky? Goopy? The precise size, shape, and appearance of your boss?

_____

_____

_____

_____

_____

_____

What's their name?

_____

Draw the little weirdo here.

Aw, they're actually kind of adorable.

THE RULE OF THREE

Sometimes—for example, if you think too hard about Jeff Bezos while simultaneously ordering a Snuggie for express delivery—your brain starts to feel like an overheating car. Use the 3-3-3 rule (an easy trick endorsed by mental health professionals) to cool it down. Here's how it works.

Write down three things you see.

1. _____

_____

2. _____

_____

3. _____

_____

Write down three things you hear.

1. _____

_____

2. _____

_____

3. _____

_____

Move three parts of your body.

Breathe deeply in and then out. Take comfort in the fact that you are here, on this planet, and that all you need to do right now is be present. Yes, you also have to take out the trash and clear out your inbox and call your mother, but you can think about that later. You have time.

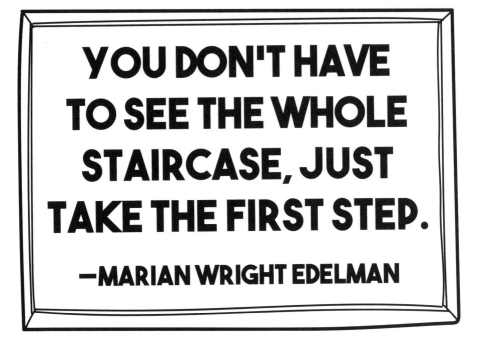

YOU DON'T HAVE TO SEE THE WHOLE STAIRCASE, JUST TAKE THE FIRST STEP.

—MARIAN WRIGHT EDELMAN

In computer-science speak, breaking down a problem is often referred to as "decomposition"—essentially just dividing what's in front of you into smaller, more manageable parts. The technique goes all the way back to René Descartes, who was (allegedly) a smart dude, so let's give his idea a shot.

What's a problem you're currently having? Big or small, it doesn't matter—this is just for practice.

_____

_____

_____

_____

_____

Now ask yourself "Why?" Write down all the possible reasons for this problem. For example, if you're having money troubles, some reasons might be "I don't get paid enough," "I spend too much money on unnecessary crap," and "I live in an expensive city."

_____

_____

_____

_____

Keep going. Break down each of the above into smaller and smaller parts by asking "Why?" Perhaps you don't get paid enough because you keep getting passed over for a raise. Again, ask yourself "Why?"

_____

_____

_____

_____

Once you've reached a place where you can no longer ask "Why," you might discover some solutions, big or small, that you can implement.

So. What's your next step?

_____

_____

_____

_____

That sounds SPECTACULAR.

GRATITUDE:
IT WORKS

When we're bummed out, the last thing we want to do is talk or write about what we're grateful for. Wallowing is much more fun. But much like taking a yoga class, as annoyed as we might be at the outset, once we've dragged ourselves through the motions, we end up realizing that yes, we do feel better.

What are some things/humans/animals/experiences/baked goods you're grateful for right this very minute?

_____

_____

_____

When was the last time someone did something kind or helpful for you that they didn't have to do?

_____

_____

_____

Can you think of anything kind or helpful you can do for a person in your life who could use some extra support? Bonus: Go do it.

_____

_____

_____

Write a thank-you note to a person in your life—your mom? Your Starbucks barista? Yourself?—who deserves one.

DEAR _____ ,

_____

_____

_____

_____

_____

_____

_____

_____

_____

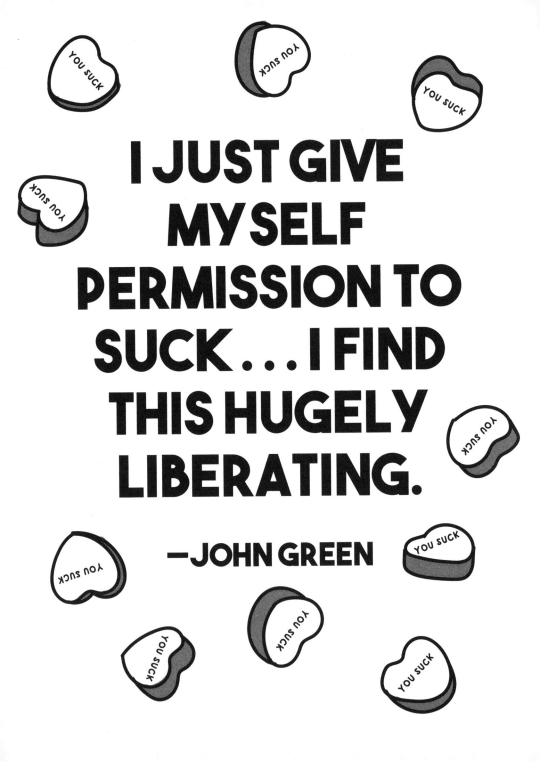

Can't hold a tune? Constantly late? No one on the planet is good at everything, except Beyoncé. People try and fail at new things all the time. Even if it turns out you never get much better, you won't know if you don't give it a shot.

What do you absolutely suck at?

_____

_____

_____

How can you celebrate the suckiest parts of you?

_____

_____

_____

And, to wrap up this exercise on a high note: What's your oddest, most obscure talent? How did you discover it?

_____

_____

_____

How do you unleash it upon the world?

_____

_____

_____

_____

THE INNER CHILD

When you were a kid, what were you afraid of?

_____

_____

_____

Do any of the patterns from your childhood still show up in your life?

_____

_____

_____

If you could go back in time and give your younger self a pep talk, what would you say?

_____

_____

_____

Now try this: Close your eyes and picture your _future_ self standing in front of you. (You look great, BTW.) What are they saying?

_____

_____

_____

_____

_____

she held herself until the sobs of the child inside subsided entirely.
I love you, she told herself.
It will all be okay.

—H. RAVEN ROSE, *SHADOW SELVES*

I WONDER IF THE SNOW *LOVES* THE TREES AND FIELDS, THAT IT KISSES THEM SO GENTLY? AND THEN IT COVERS THEM UP SNUG, YOU KNOW, WITH A WHITE QUILT; AND PERHAPS IT SAYS, "GO TO SLEEP, DARLINGS, TILL THE SUMMER COMES AGAIN."

—LEWIS CARROLL, *THROUGH THE LOOKING-GLASS*

Seasonal changes can get us down. Maybe humidity makes you nuts, or you find autumn depressing, or winter makes you want to scream "I want a beach and a piña colada and I want them now." As Pete Seeger once said (well, Ecclesiastes, but who's counting), "To everything there is a season."

Write down a few things you love, perhaps secretly, about each season.

Why winter is really quite glorious:

_____

_____

_____

Why spring is the legit best:

_____

_____

_____

Why summer should stick around forever:

_____

_____

_____

Why fall is splendid for reasons beyond pumpkin spice:

_____

_____

BOMB BATH

Baths are like the pizza of the self-care world: Even if you're "not a bath person," come on, aren't you, though?

Describe your dream evening in the bubbles. What's in the water? Are you reading? Listening to music? Mindlessly IG-scrolling and hoping you don't drop your phone? Writing in this journal?!

Set the scene.

_____

_____

_____

_____

_____

_____

Are you a book person? A device person? Do you panic about whether you're going to drop your phone in the water and have to go to the Apple store and try to convince a "genius" that your phone hasn't spent the last twenty hours in a Tupperware filled with rice?

_____

_____

_____

How about some candles? BTW, when was the last time you checked your fire alarm batteries?

_____

_____

_____

_____

_____

Now go make all those dreams a reality.

ANYONE WHO THINKS HEAVEN IS NOT HOT WATER BEHIND A LOCKED DOOR HAS FORGOTTEN WHAT IT MEANS TO LIVE.

—LUCY FRANK, *TWO GIRLS STARING AT THE CEILING*

"I NEVER IN MY LIFE," SAID TOM, "ARGUED WITH A PIECE OF CAKE OR A BOWL OF ICE CREAM."

—RAY BRADBURY, *FAREWELL SUMMER*

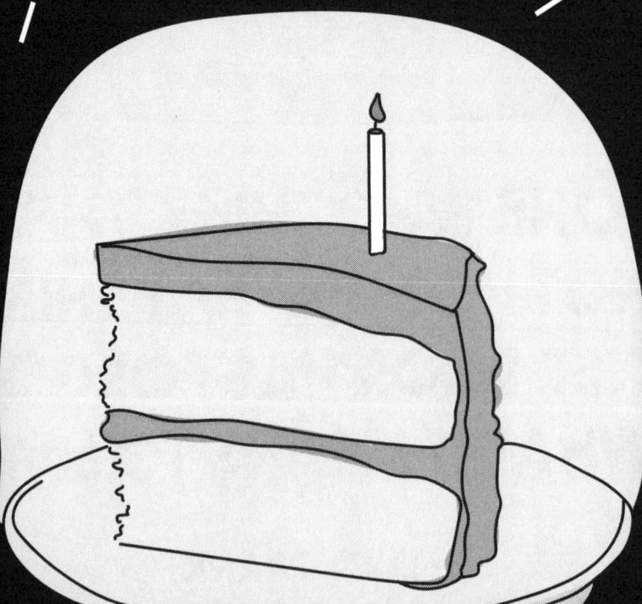

It's the simple things—a snuggle with a dog, a banana split all for yourself, Tom Holland dancing to "Umbrella" on Lip Sync Battle*— that make life wonderful. And the excellent news is that those things are everywhere. You just need to keep an eye out for them.

What are your go-to small pleasures?

_____

_____

_____

_____

_____

_____

_____

_____

_____

_____

What's something you can do right now to give yourself the equivalent of a hug?

_____

_____

_____

*If you haven't seen this, a) Who are you? and b) Go directly to The Googles. Trust.

Some sources of stress, like an overflowing inbox, are fixable. Others, like a burning and yet thwarted desire to meet and marry Timothée Chalamet and/or Zendaya, are not.

What are some sources of stress in your life?

_____

_____

_____

_____

_____

_____

_____

_____

_____

_____

_____

_____

_____

_____

Circle the ones that are fixable. Cross out the ones that aren't. Draw curly swirlies around the ones that can be fixed in the future but not right this moment.

Here's a shelf. Go ahead and put all those unfixable or not-fixable-right-now stressors on it. You can take them down later, if and when you're ready.

Emotional
Baggage
Area

STRESS IS AN IGNORANT STATE. IT BELIEVES THAT EVERYTHING IS AN EMERGENCY. NOTHING IS THAT IMPORTANT.

—NATALIE GOLDBERG

Anxiety's like a *rocking chair.* It gives you **SOMETHING TO DO,** but it doesn't *get you very far.*

—Jodi Picoult, Sing You Home

Anxiety can be a powerful motivator (see: adrenaline), but it can also get you stuck in the proverbial mud like a proverbial woolly mammoth.

Has your anxiety ever glued your proverbial feet to the floor?

_____

_____

_____

_____

_____

_____

Have you ever been able to overcome your anxiety to achieve something you never thought possible? Which of your other personal qualities came into play there?

_____

_____

_____

How do you typically deal with self-doubt and fear when they arise—besides with self-medication in Yodels form, that is?

_____

_____

_____

What's the next Big Thing you're hoping to achieve?

_____

_____

_____

What are some steps you can take to get there? Check them off as you make 'em happen.

- ☐
- ☐
- ☐
- ☐
- ☐
- ☐

FUTURE F*CKING

There's a helpful expression called "future fucking," as in, "don't future-fuck yourself." What this means: Don't catastrophize events that haven't happened or spend time obsessing over worst-case scenarios that may never come to pass. Thinking about ways that a wonderful relationship might go wrong, for example, does nothing except take you out of any happiness you're experiencing in the present.

What's one way that you sometimes future-fuck yourself?

_____

_____

_____

_____

What are some thoughts you can replace those fears with?

_____

_____

_____

_____

Now write a happy ending to the story you tend to blow out of proportion.

_____

_____

_____

_____

STEP INTO THE FUTURE AND CRUSH THOSE GOALS.

—THE JUNIOR TRAINER AT PLANET FITNESS WHO GAVE YOU THE TRAINING SESSION THAT CAME WITH MEMBERSHIP

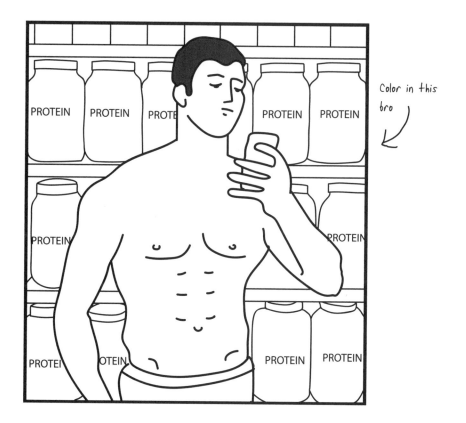

FEELINGS COME AND GO LIKE CLOUDS IN A WINDY SKY.

—Thich Nhat Hahn, *Stepping into Freedom*

Feelings are such fickle beasts. Some days it seems like you can handle anything from spilled coffee to having missed a Very Important Email from your boss, while on others the sight of a line at the ATM can send you spiraling.

Write how you're feeling today in the clouds floating across this page.

How were you feeling yesterday?

_____

_____

_____

_____

_____

_____

_____

How do you think you'll feel tomorrow?

_____

_____

_____

_____

_____

_____

_____

Bonus: Come back tomorrow and write down how you *actually* feel. It's probably not precisely how you thought you would, right? Innnteresting.

WE SPEND OUR ENTIRE LIVES TRYING TO TELL STORIES ABOUT OURSELVES— THEY'RE THE ESSENCE OF MEMORY. IT IS HOW WE MAKE LIVING IN THIS UNFEELING, ACCIDENTAL UNIVERSE TOLERABLE.

—KEN LUI, *THE PAPER MENAGERIE AND OTHER STORIES*

What story (funny, impressive, soul-crushingly mortifying, whatever) do you tend to tell when you meet someone new?

_____

_____

_____

_____

_____

_____

What's one story from your past that you feel defines you?

_____

_____

_____

_____

_____

_____

Draw the movie poster of your life here (and don't forget to give it a title that'll bring in those big international bucks).

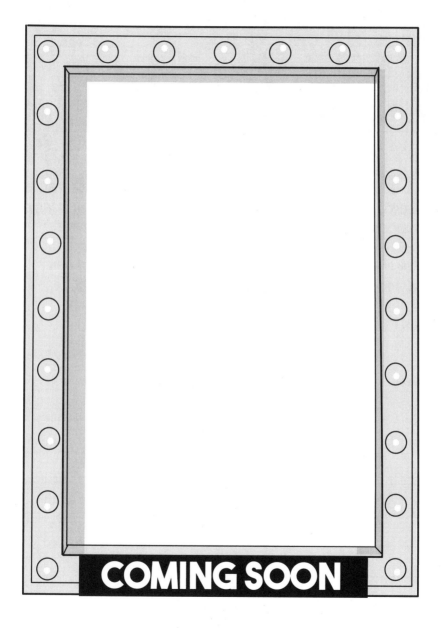

Follow your dreams.
They know the way.
–Kobi Yamada

We Anxious People tend to have some wild dreams (apocalyptic landscapes, anyone?). But even when they're flat-out horrifying in the moment, they can still give us important information about our inner selves: What we're most afraid of, what we most desire, and everything in between.

What's the last vivid dream you remember having?

_____

_____

_____

_____

_____

_____

_____

_____

_____

Whoa, that's crazy. Go ahead and analyze it here. →

_____

_____

_____

_____

_____

_____

_____

_____

What's a common theme that pops up in your dreams? What do you think it means?

_____

_____

_____

_____

_____

_____

_____

_____

_____

_____

_____

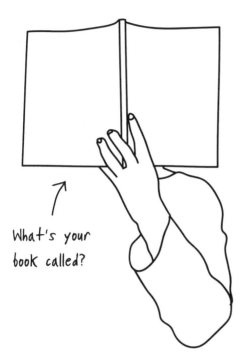

What's your book called?

There is not one big, cosmic meaning for all, there is only the meaning we each give to our life, an individual meaning, an individual plot, like an individual novel, a book for each person.

—Anaïs Nin, *The Diary of Anaïs Nin, Vol. 1: 1931-1934*

Recently, The Atlantic *columnist Arthur C. Brooks analyzed a whole bunch of studies by very smart people and determined that you can, in fact, figure out the meaning of (your) life by breaking it down into three distinct components.*

Coherence: the understanding that things in your life happen for a reason;

Purpose: the belief that you were placed on this planet for a distinct purpose, whether specific, like to write a book, or broad, like to spread love; and

Significance: the sense that your life inherently matters.

How do you see coherence fitting into your life?

_____

_____

_____

_____

What about purpose?

_____

_____

_____

_____

And finally, what about your sense of significance?

_____

_____

_____

_____

If you're experiencing a deficit in any of these areas, how do you think you could make it better?

_____

_____

_____

_____

_____

HOORAY, YOU FAILED!

Sometimes not getting the thing you thought you really, really wanted—a relationship, a job, a trip to Tahiti—turns out to be a stroke of tremendous good luck, or at least not the catastrophe that it initially appeared to be.

What's something you thought you wanted, but didn't get?

_____

_____

_____

_____

Was there any bright side to the situation? Indulging in some righteous anger counts.

_____

_____

_____

_____

Have you ever experienced a failure that ended up working out for the best—or at least not as badly as you feared?

_____

_____

_____

_____

Draw your very most loathsome ex's face here as a friendly reminder of this important principle.

WE MUST BE WILLING TO GET RID OF THE LIFE WE'VE PLANNED, SO AS TO HAVE THE LIFE THAT IS WAITING FOR US.

—JOSEPH CAMPBELL

Remember when you were a kid and you wanted to be a taxi driver/president of the United States/astronaut all at the same time? But you now realize that if you were a taxi driver, you'd have been outsourced to Uber; that being president of the United States sounds exhausting; and that astronauts have to wear diapers? #crisisaverted #whew

What did you want to be when you grew up?

_____

Does that still sound like a good idea? Why/why not?

_____

_____

Does anything about your current profession reflect what you wanted to be when you were a kid?*

_____

_____

_____

*If the answer is "No," that's okay. The authors of this book wanted to be a florist and a Gap salesperson and are now a professional plant-killer and a slob, respectively. All's well that ends well.

What's your current dream job? How would having it change your life for the better?

_____

_____

_____

_____

_____

_____

_____

_____

_____

_____

_____

_____

_____

_____

_____

_____

_____

_____

Actual still from the movie, obvi.

Breaking news: You can't control the past; it already happened. Which leads to the necessary conclusion that regrets amount to nothing more than a waste of your fucking time. Remember that Ashton Kutcher movie where every decision he made had an impact on every single moment of the rest of his life? (It's called The Butterfly Effect *and it is equal parts terrible and amazing, as most Ashton Kutcher movies are.) The point is that you can't untangle anything about your past from the rest of the big, weird tapestry that is your life. Listen to Ashton, get over that shitty decision you made when you were eighteen, and move on.*

Write about a time when something, small or big, happened that felt like it changed *everything*.

_____

_____

_____

_____

_____

_____

_____

_____

_____

_____

LET GO OF THE ILLUSION THAT IT COULD HAVE HAPPENED ANY OTHER WAY. —UNKNOWN

What kinds of butterfly effects did this event have in your life? What can you imagine happening in the future because this one thing occurred?

_____

_____

_____

_____

_____

_____

_____

_____

_____

_____

_____

_____

MINDFULNESS, SURE

Just reading the word "mindfulness" may make you want to rage-tweet @goop, and we get it: The media saturation is real. We all know by now that "being present" is so! important! And of course it is. But it's also not always possible—like, say, if you're working overtime on an insane deadline because you need money because capitalism, and taking a break to quiet your mind is just not on this moment's particular menu.

What are your feelings about mindfulness? Frustration? Adoration? Nausea? Let them out; Gwyneth will never know.

_____

_____

_____

_____

_____

Do you have any practices to help you live in the moment? ASMR on YouTube? Chakra-locating crystals? Hanging up rustic wooden signs from HomeGoods that say "Dance like no one's watching" around your house?

_____

_____

_____

_____

_____

If cultivating more mindfulness sounds appealing, how do you think you could incorporate it into your life, even in the tiniest of ways?

_____

_____

_____

_____

_____

_____

Add your very own motivational sign to the gallery wall below. Bonus: Sell it to HomeGoods and make those millions.

I guess I'm gonna fade into Bolivian.

-Mike Tyson

I love the smell of diapers...

-Sarah Jessica Parker

WE ARE ALL IN THE GUTTER, BUT SOME OF US ARE LOOKING AT THE STARS.

—OSCAR WILDE, *LADY WINDERMERE'S FAN*

Perspective: It's so useful! Like, for example, say the power goes out on Thanksgiving and you were planning to host, but now you have to cancel. That's sad, because gravy is delicious. It's also great, because now you can throw down a glass of full-bodied Cab with notes of cherry and damp barnyard while eating Chinese takeout and not listening to your dad's opinion of Anderson Cooper. Also, when the power goes out, you can see the stars.

See how that works?

What's a problem you've been struggling with lately?

_____

_____

_____

_____

Is there any way to reframe this problem? Any upsides?

_____

_____

_____

What's the worst, most catastrophic possible outcome?

_____

_____

_____

What would you do if that happened?

_____

_____

_____

Finally, how much control do you have over whether this does or does not happen?

_____

_____

_____

If the answer is "A lot, as it turns out!," what are some steps you can put into place?

_____

_____

_____

If the answer is "Ugh, none" . . . see pages 38–39. And then let that shit go.

GLAD TO BE HERE

Our world can feel like (is?) a dumpster fire, and the stress associated with the ever-present news cycle is overwhelming, to say the least. So let's play "Why 'right now' isn't the actual worst, even though it feels like it"!

What are some past eras you're psyched not to be living in?*
Why?

_____

_____

_____

_____

_____

*If you have trouble getting started, a few factoids:

In the ancient Roman Empire, slavery was a big business due to the pressing need for aqueducts. Shockingly, those enslaved humans weren't treated especially well, and were from time to time thrown into pits to be devoured by wild animals, because sure.

In 536 AD, a volcanic eruption blackened the sky, leaving the earth cold and dark for EIGHTEEN MONTHS.

Castles of the Middle Ages frequently tucked cesspools for human waste under the floorboards. In 1184, during an event at the Petersburg Citadel in Erfurt hosted by King Henry VI, the floor of the main hall broke, resulting in upwards of sixty dinner guests drowning in literal shit. The King, in keeping with the Western world's long-standing preference for rich white men, survived.

Here are a few A++ things about today's world:

Dolly Parton exists

So do public libraries

Thanks to that thing permanently attached to your hand, you will always know where the closest gas station is

Scotland's national animal is the unicorn

Now add your own.

_____

_____

_____

_____

_____

_____

_____

_____

_____

_____

_____

_____

THE MOST IMPORTANT REASON FOR GOING FROM ONE PLACE TO ANOTHER IS TO SEE WHAT'S IN BETWEEN, AND THEY TOOK GREAT PLEASURE IN DOING JUST THAT.

—NORTON JUSTER,
THE PHANTOM TOLLBOOTH

Sure, getting the raise you deserve, signing the lease on a rent-controlled apartment, and embarking on a mutually satisfying love affair involving no ghosting whatsoever are all events worth celebrating, but life isn't just about leaping from Big Moment to Big Moment. It's about paying attention to, and appreciating, all those cool fun-sized things in between.

Write down all the teeny-tiny parts of today that made you happy here:

△ _____

△ _____

△ _____

△ _____

△ _____

△ _____

△ _____

△ _____

△ _____

Now doodle some of them over here:

SPLIT THIS

Leaving the house: It's the worst. Anything is better than an evening interacting with random acquaintances, at the end of which you are presented with a $84 check for your Diet Coke and cup of lentil soup because "It's easier to just split it."

Who is the number one person you absolutely cannot stand right now?

_____

_____

_____

Spill it: What happened last time you went out with them?

_____

_____

_____

_____

_____

_____

_____

_____

_____

_____

If you went out to dinner with them at the fanciest restaurant on the planet tonight, what would you order and then make them pay for? Add whatever you want to the check below; it's on them.

GUEST CHECK

DATE	SERVER	TABLE	GUESTS	CHECK NUMBER
				681659
			TAX		
			TOTAL		

Thank You - Please Come Again

thanks, hon

ZITS AND CLIQUES AND GEOMETRY TESTS, OH MY

Middle school is a hotbed of pure, unadulterated misery for everyone—yes, even Kaitlin, who seemingly sailed through junior high on a cloud of acne-free skin and sports-related accolades. Everyone!

How was your middle school experience? Try to be more descriptive than "bad." We already know it was bad.

_____

_____

_____

_____

_____

_____

What would you like to say to the person who was most determined to make your life miserable?

_____

_____

_____

_____

_____

_____

In addition to Taco Tuesday, videos of cats squeezing into impossibly small containers, and blackout curtains, who or what made your days better back then?

_____

_____

_____

_____

_____

_____

_____

Check off your favorite taco toppings from the exhaustive list below, then top your taco.*

EXHAUSTIVE LIST
OF TACO TOPPINGS:

- ☐ Cheese
- ☐ Lettuce
- ☐ Salsa
- ☐ Onion
- ☐ Beans
- ☐ Cilantro
- ☐ Jalapeno
- ☐ Guacamole
- ☐ Sour cream
- ☐ Pico de gallo
- ☐ Mango
- ☐ Olives
- ☐ Doritos
- ☐ Lime

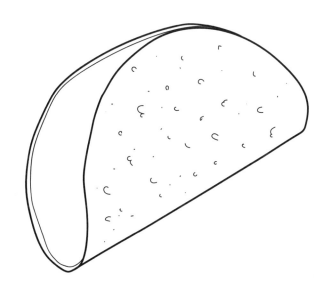

*Sounds dirty. Didn't mean it that way. Maybe.

UNCLUTTERED

Marie Kondo has taught us that a life sans clutter is a joyful one. She also recommends an intricate sock-folding method to keep your . . . socks . . . from getting . . . stressed. Which, sure.

But! There's a case to be made for stressed-out socks. If you stopped worrying about all the nagging little things you have to do around the house, what would you do with all that extra space in your brain?

What steps can you take to lower your expectations about the state of your junk drawer?

_____

_____

_____

_____

_____

_____

_____

Right here, right now, can you commit to never again watching TikToks featuring white women named Melanie putting their snack food into clear acrylic containers labeled "snack food" and then storing the original snack food bags somewhere out of sight because they do not fit their aesthetic?

_____ Yes   _____ No, those are the best

Why or why not?

_____

_____

_____

_____

_____

_____

GO THE FUCK TO SLEEP

Ever suffer from insomnia? Hahahaha, that was a joke because you are at this very moment holding a journal for Anxious People in your hot little hands. (Nice cuticles, BTW.*)

What are some of the things you think about when you can't go to sleep?

_____

_____

_____

_____

_____

_____

Besides "writing down what's on your mind in a journal next to your bed" (which sometimes but doesn't always work), any thoughts on what you might be able to try next time it's three a.m. and you're staring at the beastly numbers on your phone?

_____

_____

_____

_____

_____

*Another joke.

Has your insomnia ever led to anything productive? Mainlining a bowl of straight whipped cream at dawn counts.

_____

_____

_____

_____

_____

_____

_____

Decorate the eye mask that you very much need.

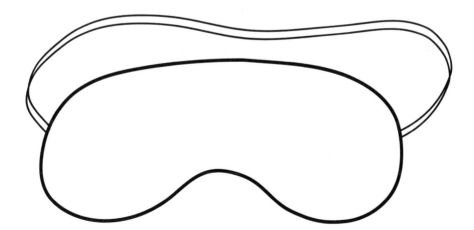

WORRYING IS CARRYING TOMORROW'S LOAD WITH TODAY'S STRENGTH— CARRYING TWO DAYS AT ONCE. IT IS MOVING INTO TOMORROW AHEAD OF TIME. WORRYING DOESN'T EMPTY TOMORROW OF ITS SORROW, IT EMPTIES TODAY OF ITS STRENGTH.

—CORRIE TEN BOOM, *CLIPPINGS FROM MY NOTEBOOK*

Worries can be helpful, like if you were worried about getting fired for always being late to work and, as a result, made a point of getting in more or less on time. But sometimes we get hung up on issues that we can't really do anything about, like Aunt Clarice's political views.

Write down something that's bothering you but that is completely out of your control on this (biodegradable) paper right here and imagine dropping it into the ocean below.

LESS IS MORE, UNLESS IT'S KINDNESS, SLEEP, OR TOILET PAPER.

—UNKNOWN

There are some things (almost) all of us want more of: Money. Travel. Abs. But when we take off our consumer goggles, we might discover that there are unexpected blessings we already have in abundance. Like, remember how when you were a kid all you wanted was to be able to do whatever you felt like doing? And now you technically can, and you don't even have any homework?!

Like that, minus the fact that you now also have to pay for things like car insurance and electricity.

What do you have in abundance?

_____

_____

_____

_____

_____

_____

What do you want more of?

_____

_____

_____

_____

_____

_____

What do you want less of?

_____

_____

_____

_____

_____

_____

What do you have the exact perfect amount of?

_____

_____

_____

_____

_____

THE ONLY
TOXIC

WE'RE WELCOMING INTO
OUR LIVES RIGHT NOW

You know that toxic person in your circle? The one who contributes virtually nothing positive to your daily existence but who consumes an inordinate amount of your headspace?

Yeah, that person.

What about them do you think gets under your skin so much?

_____

_____

_____

_____

_____

_____

_____

Draw them on this outline over here and then scribble them right on out. You don't need that shit in your life.

STEP AWAY FROM THE INK

There is a thing you should not do when you are in a crap headspace, and it is called Body Modification of Any Sort At All.

Draw the tattoo you are not going to get until you feel less anxious.

Now list some nonpermanent ways to boost your mood (a hot new graphic novel! A hot new set of throw pillows! A hot new weighted blanket!) here.

A comfy thing: _____

A thing I can buy to release endorphins: _____

A thing that's nice to hear: _____

A thing that's nice to look at: _____

A thing that feels good: _____

A thing that tastes good: _____

A thing that smells good: _____

A thing I want to squeeze: _____

A thing that makes me relaxed: _____

A thing I want to watch: _____

A thing I want to create: _____

A thing I want to read: _____

A thing I want to do: _____

A thing that never, ever fails to make me smile: _____

DUMPSTER FIRE

We all have anxieties that are super particular to us, as you likely know, since you are currently holding this book. These anxieties can range from the highly understandable (MoveOn.org updates) to the decidedly odd (fun fact: Tyra Banks is allegedly terrified of dolphins).

What were the last five things that made you anxious?

_____

_____

_____

What do you think triggered those fears? Too much coffee? Too little sleep? Childhood experiences? Really try to get at the root issues here.

_____

_____

_____

_____

Is there anything you can do to avoid those triggers in the future?

_____

_____

_____

_____

Now toss those five things that make you anxious into this raging pit of chaos. Ah, so much better.

THROW COMPLIMENTS

Give your dog a compliment.

_____

_____

_____

Give your best friend a compliment.

_____

_____

_____

Give your pillow a compliment.

_____

_____

_____

Easy, right? Now give a compliment to Carol from HR.

_____

_____

. . . Harder.

There are some creatures in your life that it's easy to be kind to and others that make your Grinchy heart shrink to the size of a Tic Tac. But! You can think of something *nice to say about (almost) everyone.*

LIKE AIRPLANES

Go ahead, fill these paper airplanes with compliments for the people in your life who may not be your *favorites*, but come on: Everyone deserves to have a kind word said about them.

Everyone is born creative; everyone is given a box of crayons in kindergarten. Then when you hit puberty they take the crayons away . . . Being suddenly hit years later with the "creative bug" is just a wee voice telling you, "I'd like my crayons back, please."

—Hugh MacLeod, *Ignore Everybody*

Fill in this beautiful, blank circle with your very own design.

What's your favorite creative or creative-adjacent hobby? Home repair? Cooking? Writing in your *Big Journal for Anxious People*?!?! It all counts.

_____

_____

_____

_____

_____

_____

What's the most creative gift you've ever given?

_____

_____

_____

_____

_____

_____

What's the best homemade gift you've ever received?

_____

_____

_____

_____

_____

_____

LIFE MOVES PRETTY *FAST.* IF YOU DON'T STOP AND LOOK AROUND ONCE IN A WHILE, YOU COULD MISS IT.

—FERRIS BUELLER'S DAY OFF

Most of us spend a lot of time focusing on the future: What we want, how to get it, what we're lacking in the meantime. It's extremely stressful, and it also keeps us from noticing all the rad stuff that's happening in the middle of our story (aka the part we're in right now).

Like, say you want to take a road trip. That sounds fun! But part of the fun is also the process: Picking where you want to go, researching restaurants, getting excited with your travel partners. In other words, it's not all about the finish line.

What's a long-term goal of yours?

_____

_____

_____

_____

_____

_____

What are you doing to get there?

_____

_____

_____

_____

_____

_____

What's surprisingly fun or interesting about the process of getting to that goal?

_____

_____

_____

_____

_____

_____

BIG EMPATHY

Have you ever tripped and been absolutely certain that everyone within five hundred yards both saw you and is currently mocking you? The truth is, people spend a lot less time thinking about us and our fuckups than we imagine. Most people, in fact, aren't thinking about us at all.

Why is it important to realize this? Not only does it take a lot of the pressure off, considering what might be on other people's minds can increase your empathy for them and what they *might be going through—which, again, very likely has absolutely nothing to do with you.*

Now think back to a time when someone said something hurtful to you. Is it possible that they were hurting, too? What might have been going on with them?

_____

_____

_____

_____

_____

_____

_____

_____

_____

_____

Have you ever said something hurtful to someone that you didn't mean? Why do you think you said it?

_____

_____

_____

_____

_____

_____

What are these people thinking about? (Hint: It's not you.)

MORNING DUMP

Taking a few minutes to journal in the morning is the mental equivalent of taking a much-needed poop: It gets rid of all the shit that might be bogging you down. It might bring to light things that you didn't even know were on your mind—and once they're out there on paper, you can deal with them. Take ten minutes (just ten! You can do it!) and practice externalizing your inner monologue here.

_____

_____

_____

_____

_____

_____

_____

_____

_____

_____

_____

_____

_____

_____

Freedom is not the absence of commitments, but the ability to choose—and commit myself to—what is best for me.

–Paulo Coelho, *The Zahir*

When we're looking to make a big life change—whether that's quitting drinking, going to the gym we're already paying for, or never again going to Target "just to look"—it can be easy to come down hard on ourselves for any perceived setback. Shouldn't we be more *disciplined* than that?!

The key word here is "discipline." To wit: When you think of "discipline," what comes to mind? Maybe being sent to the principal's office because you tried to staple Maisie's finger to your fingerpaint masterpiece (what?! She *asked* you to!), or your friend who's constantly trying one trendy diet or another and is constantly miserable (and constantly talking about it)?

Discipline, in other words, is all about "No, you can't." Discipline says, "You will *not* eat that burrito because if you do you are worthless and spineless and lazy and destined to die alone." This is not especially encouraging, nor is it a super fun way to live.

Which brings us to "commitment," a much kinder bedfellow. Commitment *wants* you to succeed. When you slip and fall, commitment helps you up.

What are some things you try to be "disciplined" about? How can you reframe these into commitments?

RULE	COMMITMENT
I will never again stay up past midnight on a weekday to watch *Bridgerton*.	I value my health and sanity, and I commit to getting a better night's sleep. Also, I can watch *Bridgerton* whenever I want, like while eating breakfast, because nothing goes with horny British socialites like oatmeal.

DIY HAPPY PLACE

Everybody has a happy place. Maybe yours is sitting on a rowboat in the middle of a lake with the sun on your face. Or maybe it's sitting in bed with Love Is Blind *on autoplay and last night's leftovers on your lap. Whatever works.*

When you picture yourself somewhere truly blissful, where in the world are you?

_____

_____

_____

What are you doing, if anything?

_____

_____

_____

What are you wearing, if anything?

_____

_____

_____

What are you listening to, if anything?

_____

_____

_____

Is there anyone else there (baby bunnies count)?

_____

_____

_____

If there's a TV, what series are you watching in its entirety?

_____

_____

_____

What's on the menu (which shan't be cooked by you)?

_____

_____

_____

Where will your first nap be taking place?

_____

_____

_____

Which hot and spicy celebrity is applying lotion to your feet?

_____

_____

_____

JUST SAY NO
(TO LOTS AND LOTS OF CAFFEINE)

Obviously, mainlining espresso doesn't do wonders for the ol' anxiety, but all sorts of substances that we do (or don't) put into our body can have a surprisingly dramatic impact on how we're feeling over the course of a day.

To get a handle on what foods and drinks might either trigger or lessen your anxiety, try keeping a journal for a day. Mark down what you consumed in the left column and how you felt afterward on the right.

Consumed...	Felt like...
Spaghetti	A yeti

Design the enormous energy drink you shan't be consuming today.

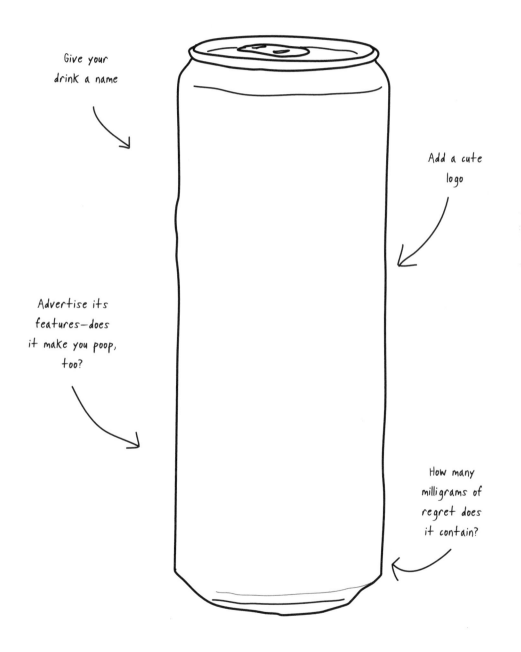

Give your drink a name

Add a cute logo

Advertise its features—does it make you poop, too?

How many milligrams of regret does it contain?

I HAVE NO SPECIAL TALENT, BUT AM ONLY PASSIONATELY CURIOUS.

—ALBERT EINSTEIN

Everyone's good at something. *Maybe you're excellent at avoiding going to the DMV! Or you almost always make it to the front of the line at Dunkin' Donuts without having a panic attack! Hey, you got out of bed this morning! That's talent.*

What would you win your medals for? Come on, don't be shy.

Did you ever win a for-real medal? What for?

_____

_____

_____

(RE) FRAME IT

One of the most infuriating by-products of anxiety is that it inspires all sorts of catastrophic and usually unrealistic thoughts about what *might* happen. For example, if you're anxious about a first date, your brain might start posting an emergency warning titled, "THEY ARE GOING TO THINK YOU'RE A BEAST JUST CANCEL IT NOWWWW."

The more logical line of thought: It may not be love at first sight, but chances are your date will not run away shrieking at the first sight of your beastliness.

The problem is that our brains aren't always great at overriding our emergency warning systems, which brings us to a strategy called "reframing." Reframing is essentially training yourself to look at a situation that makes you anxious from a different—and likely more realistic—perspective.

What's a future event that's causing you anxiety?

_____

_____

Write down any unrealistic and/or catastrophic feelings about this event here.	Now, over here, reframe each of those thoughts into a more logical, realistic outcome.

LIKE APPLE TV+ BUT FOR YOUR BRAIN

Wouldn't it be swell if life was like a TiVo (RIP)? We could click away from the not-so-hot moments, rewind and rewatch the epic ones, and just throw the whole damn thing on pause (or off! #imagine) whenever we needed a bathroom break.

Label the buttons on this remote with all the things you wish you could do to your brain, which needs to stop *This Is Us* and pivot to *Schitt's Creek* STAT.

"If I could turn back tiiime, if I could find a way . . . ," I would:

_____

_____

_____

_____

_____

_____

_____

_____

_____

_____

> You empower what you fight. You withdraw power from what you release.
>
> –Alan Cohen

When was the last time you had a good, hard cry?

_____

_____

_____

_____

_____

When was the last time you held back tears?

_____

_____

_____

_____

When was the last time you comforted someone who was crying?

_____

_____

_____

_____

_____

_____

What song/movie/book/other glorious work of art is guaranteed to turn on the waterworks? Why do you think that is?

_____

_____

_____

_____

_____

_____

How do you feel about crying? Embarrassed? Relieved? Like your face is very wet?

_____

_____

_____

_____

_____

_____

PIECE BY PIECE

Collaging: It's not just for preschoolers and your mother-in-law with her extensive collection of craft-store coupons. The marvelous thing about collaging is that you don't even need a concept: You can just start cutting and pasting and see what it evolves into. What a wonderful approach to art, and to life.

Go ahead and grab some glue and magazines (or junk mail, wrapping paper, tissues soggy with the tears of existential malaise, whatever) and give it a shot. PS: If you don't have glue, you can make a flour-water paste.

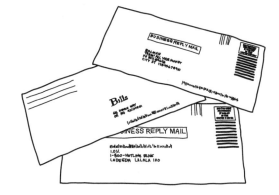

> # Temper tantrums, however fun they may be to throw, rarely solve whatever problem is causing them.
>
> —Lemony Snicket, *Horseradish*

Have you ever seen a toddler have a truly Exorcist-*level temper tantrum, complete with floor collapses and screams that seem more suited to a slow, tortuous death than, say, the fact that there are no more Cheerios?*

The reason toddlers have these kinds of meltdowns is quite simple: They've started to get a taste of what control feels like. They can say "Yes," say "No," pick things up by themselves, and so forth, and so when that control is taken from them ("No, you can't have any more Cheerios"), they super do not enjoy it. They express that lack of enjoyment the only way they know how: By losing their shit.

When we feel a lack of control in our lives—hi, daily existence as a human being on planet Earth!—we may feel our inner toddler begin to emerge, whether it be through road rage or DEFCON 1 Twitter rants. But control is mainly an illusion. There are, of course, many things we can control, but many, many more that we can't—and that realization can be such a relief. (A three-year-old-style temper tantrum is permissible once in a while, too; just try not to hurt or terrify anyone, K?)

What are some things you can control in your life?

_____

_____

_____

_____

_____

_____

_____

_____

_____

What are some that you can't?

_____

_____

_____

_____

_____

_____

_____

_____

_____

_____

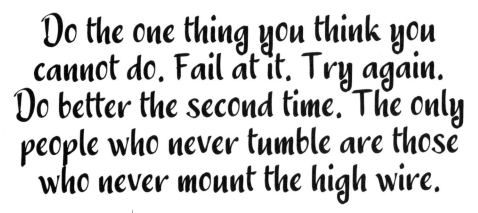

Do the one thing you think you cannot do. Fail at it. Try again. Do better the second time. The only people who never tumble are those who never mount the high wire.

—Lady O

As anyone who loves Oprah (aka everyone) knows, imagining the life you want can have a profound effect on your reality.

What do you want to invite more of into your life?

This person → _____

This place → _____

This practice → _____

This knowledge → _____

This feeling → _____

Mostly, more of this please → _____

And less of this, thanks → _____

Use this page to craft a mood board for your future—doodle, draw, write, collage, whatever feels right—and then vision that shit into existence.

TEENY-TINY BUCKET LIST

Some people make a big fuss about their bucket lists—climbing Everest, reading the collected works of Shakespeare, making out with Idris Elba—but while these major goals are great, they can distract us from the small accomplishments that come with each and every day, from tidying a drawer to spending a solid, uninterrupted hour with a good book.

What are five things you can put on your bucket list for just today?

1. _____

2. _____

3. _____

4. _____

5. _____

What are five things you can put on your bucket list for this week?

1. _____

2. _____

3. _____

4. _____

5. _____

FOR THE GREAT DOESN'T HAPPEN THROUGH IMPULSE ALONE, AND IS A SUCCESSION OF LITTLE THINGS THAT ARE BROUGHT TOGETHER.

—VINCENT VAN GOGH

My Bucket List
by Vincent V. G.
1. Only smoke
pipe seven times.
2. Glass of water
3. Leave append-
ages intact

A FEELINGS RAINBOW

Color in this rainbow. Which words do you associate with the colors below?

Red: _____

Orange: _____

Yellow: _____

Green: _____

Blue: _____

Pink: _____

Purple: _____

Black: _____

White: _____

Chromotherapy, or color therapy, is based on the belief that colors can have an effect on physical and/or mental health, and that you should bring them into your space accordingly.

When you look around your space, what colors do you see the most of?

_____

_____

_____

_____

How do those colors make you feel?

_____

_____

_____

_____

Based on your feelings rainbow, which colors could you use a little more of in your life? How might you make that happen?

_____

_____

_____

_____

_____

TIME YOU ENJOY WASTING IS NOT WASTED TIME.

—MARTHE TROLY-CURTIN, *PHRYNETTE MARRIED*

e.g., time spent snuggling puppies

Time-wasting: One of life's most underrated pursuits. Society places such enormous emphasis on constant achievement that we can forget how lovely it is to do, well, nothing. And if you need more encouragement next time you feel like spending an afternoon in the company of Andy Cohen and your cat, remember that research shows that periodic disconnection improves productivity, because it gives your brain the equivalent of a weekend in Cabo.

How do you feel about the concept of "wasting time"? Stressed out? Relieved? Overjoyed at the mere thought?

_____

_____

_____

_____

_____

_____

_____

What were some of your favorite ways to waste time as a kid?

_____

_____

_____

_____

_____

_____

What about now?

_____

_____

_____

_____

_____

How can you make room for more time-wasting in your life?

_____

_____

_____

_____

_____

_____

REFLECTION IS THE PROCESS THAT TURNS EXPERIENCE INTO INSIGHT.

– JOHN C. MAXWELL

Think back to one year ago. What was your life like?

_____

_____

_____

_____

_____

_____

_____

_____

_____

How have you changed?

_____

_____

_____

_____

_____

_____

How have your circumstances changed?

_____

_____

_____

_____

_____

What are some changes that you're grateful for?

_____

_____

_____

_____

_____

_____

TAKE A SHOWER, WASH OFF THE DAY. DRINK A GLASS OF WATER. MAKE THE ROOM DARK. LIE DOWN AND CLOSE YOUR EYES. NOTICE THE SILENCE. NOTICE YOUR HEART. STILL BEATING. STILL FIGHTING. YOU MADE IT, AFTER ALL. YOU MADE IT, ANOTHER DAY. AND YOU CAN MAKE IT ONE MORE. YOU'RE DOING JUST FINE.

—CHARLOTTE ERIKSSON, "YOU'RE DOING JUST FINE"

Use these pages to write a letter to your future self. What are your hopes and dreams for this person?

_____

_____

_____

_____

_____

_____

_____

_____

_____

_____

_____

_____

_____

_____

_____

_____

_____

_____

_____